Rediscovering You!
How to be a Proverbs 31 Woman in a Modern Day World

Alexandria Nsenga

Copyright © 2023 Alexandria Nsenga

All rights reserved.

ISBN: 979-8-86-642792-5

To my beautiful, brave and bold daughter Savannah, I pray that you will know from an early age how amazing you are and how fearfully and wonderfully made God created you to be.

To my mom, Granny and all the strong women in my family, mentors and close friends, I am thankful God placed you in my life and that you are amazing examples of women of Faith.

To the reader, I also dedicate this book to you. We are on this journey together and no matter where you are in life, I know that God is not done with you yet! So, let's keep moving forward together, sis.

CONTENTS

	Acknowledgments	i
	Introduction	1
1	Proverbs 31:10	Pg # 4
2	Proverbs 31:11-12	Pg # 13
3	Proverbs 31:13-19	Pg # 19
4	Proverbs 31:20	Pg # 25
5	Proverbs 31:21	Pg # 30
6	Proverbs 31:22-24	Pg # 34
7	Proverbs 31:25-26	Pg #40
8	Proverbs 31:27-29	Pg # 45
9	Proverbs 31:30-31	Pg # 48

ACKNOWLEDGMENTS

I want to start by thanking my wonderful husband, Mandela. Thank you for being my number one supporter, believing in me and always encouraging me to follow what God puts on my heart to do. I love you so much. Thank you to my Auntie Jenny for helping me edit this book, your knowledge and expertise has helped me immensely in making this book be the best it can be. Thank you to my dear friend Katy, for shooting the cover of this book. You have captivated the essence of what I want this book to be about. You have a beautiful gift that God has given you. Thank you to my mom Jackie and my sister Keonna for cheering me on and always being in my corner. Finally, to my mentors Ingrid and Janice, thank you for your deep love and support in my journey of faith and for always pointing me to Jesus. You have helped me to be confident in hearing His voice, which has led me to share with others what He has been speaking to me through this book.

INTRODUCTION

When I hear about the Proverbs 31 woman, what generally comes to my mind is, "WOW! This woman is the full definition of a boss babe!" But seriously! She does it all! She cooks, she cleans, she creates, she invests, she multiplies, she gives… she is superwoman… and then when I think of that, I think to myself, "Yup…well, good for her! I won't ever be able to do all of THAT…..back to binge-watching The Bachelor!" And we tend to leave it at that. We may take pieces of verses and apply it to our lives. But I have discovered, that the Proverbs 31 woman we read about in the bible, is not just meant to be admired, but is meant to be an example to all of us women as well! She is meant to be an encouragement and an inspiration where we can follow in her footsteps! What if I were to tell you that you can BE that Proverbs 31 woman. That you ARE that woman. The woman God created YOU to be. I want to invite you into this series as we rediscover what it truly means to be a Proverbs 31 woman in the 21st century. You are made to thrive not just survive. You are made to be a woman who is strong and is a blessing to others. You are made as a precious and gifted daughter of the most high God.

Here's a bit of a back story before we jump right into the traits of this Proverbs 31 woman. See, at the beginning of the chapter it is actually addressing King Lemuel's mom who I think is full of wisdom and she sits him down and is giving him the rundown on life. But she specifically narrows in on him finding a wife for 21 verses!!! Why so much emphasis on this? I believe it's because in life, we are not meant to do it alone. We are not meant to be isolated. Males AND females are not meant to live life alone, or even separately. That doesn't mean you have to get married. But there is value in working and partnering together, in whatever form that looks like. In the Bible, I see from the beginning how God created Adam and Eve to partner in life, all the way to where Paul partners in ministry with mighty women of God such as Priscilla and Aquilla. Paul actually refers to these two women as his co-workers. It is of great value when we work together.

In life, human beings are of the utmost importance. That is why in Genesis 2:7, it talks about God breathing life into us. Genesis 2:7 says, *"Then the Lord God formed a man from the dust of the ground and breathed into his nostrils the breath of life, and the man became a living being." (NIV)*

He didn't breathe life into anything else. He commanded everything else to come to be. But with us, he breathed his own breath of life into us. It was personal for God. He wants to literally live in and through us. Why? Because He is crazy about you. He loves you and has chosen YOU do to mighty and powerful things through here on Earth.

God is crazy about all of us because his very own living breath is inside each one of us. I think about my son and my daughter and how every time I see them, I can't help but feel proud, I can't help but love on them so much! Why? Because I am looking at my very own DNA! My blood is running through them and I can't help but be in awe. I believe God feels the same way about us. And I would hope that my kids grow to become best friends, to love each other, to live life together and support each other through their ups and downs. God wants us to work together, live life on Earth and have dominion over the earth together! He didn't create us to be in competition with one another. We are His children! He wants us to be united. I believe King Lemuel's mom was really explaining the added value a woman is to a man's life. We are special, we are valuable, and we are needed. So throughout the rest of this book, I will be breaking down who this Proverbs 31 woman is, why she is so amazing, and how we can live out this amazing and honorable life, just as she did. I pray you feel empowered, encouraged and strengthened after reading this. Let's go girls!

CHAPTER 1

Proverbs 31:10

"Who can find a virtuous and capable wife? She is more precious than rubies." (NLT)

Now, some versions say who can find a virtuous and capable *woman*. This really does apply to all women, not just wives. It speaks of a woman who is excellent in her character. An amazing description I read said this: "A virtuous woman knows how to grab heaven and apply it to earth so that life is better for everyone in her influence."

As women, we tend to wear many hats. Some of us are wives, daughters, moms, sisters, caretakers, career women, leaders, teachers…the list goes on and on. Maybe you identify with some of these titles, and maybe you identify with all of them! I just want to stop right here and applaud you. You are amazing. Women can multitask and do so much because we wear so many hats. It is not easy! So you go girl. I am for you!

Since this virtuous woman gives so much to everyone around her (due to the many hats she wears), she not only gives but does it in a way that is highly valuable in God's eyes. When I kept thinking about the word virtuous, I needed to have some more background-because virtuous seemed like such a fancy word where you know what it means, but at the same time if someone asked you, it would be hard to explain. So, some other words for virtuous are:

Good

Righteous

Ethical

Pure

Honest

Nice

True

Having high moral standards

Think of a woman in your life that embodies this. Maybe you need to write it down or even send her a text and just honor her by telling her how amazing you think she is! Let's continue to encourage each other by actually telling each other how awesome we are.

Okay great! Now that you've done that, think about this person you look up to. Why do you admire her so much. Do you believe that you can exude these characteristics like this woman does?

If you have any doubt in your mind, that's okay. We are human, and we don't always think highly of ourselves. Yes, we make mistakes, but that does not mean we don't have purpose and that God does not want to use us. To the woman who feels like she won't ever be the "woman" she wants to be, I want to tell you that God loves you right now with his whole heart. Just the way you are right now. Rest in His love. Yes, He refines us and purifies us and helps us be the best we can be, but enjoy the journey. It's in the journey where we really get to know Jesus more intimately.

The Hebrew word for virtuous woman is 'Eshet Chayil'. Eshet, also referred to as isha, means woman. Chayil means bravery, capability, triumphant, rampart and wealth.

Eshet Chayil represents virtues of courage and strength. As I studied this, I realized that a Proverbs 31 woman is a mighty warrior. It doesn't mean she's not afraid, she just chooses to press on despite the fear. She does it afraid. She doesn't shy away from adversity, instead she chooses to face it head on.

A virtuous woman is a fighter. She's resilient. She never gives up. A virtuous woman is not a perfect woman. I think many times, especially for Christian women, we tend to think that the virtuous woman is the ideal, 'perfect' woman. I don't think she is perfect. Only Jesus is perfect. She could have been battling depression. She could have been struggling with anxiety or jealousy. We don't know her inner struggles. But what we do know is that she is a warrior, and she kept pushing through. She got up every morning despite how she felt and took care of her household. She operated her own business with wisdom and grace. She loved on her husband and children. She made those choices everyday despite how she felt. In her own strength? No, but because of the strength that comes from one person, Jesus Christ.

You may not always feel like a virtuous woman. But you are. Why? Because when we accept Jesus as our personal Lord and Savior, we become daughters. Daughters of a King. Daughters of a most high God who gives us strength, and who IS our strength. So, we are virtuous because of Jesus. Jesus is our strength and courage.

If you haven't accepted Jesus into your heart, I want to take time right now to give you the opportunity. I will purposely pause writing this book to take a moment to extend the best invitation you will ever receive. It is that important. See, Jesus Christ is perfect. Because He is perfect, we don't have to be. He took the pressure off of us and put it on himself. He died on a cross and rose from the grave to save you from your sins so that you could live with Him forever in eternity. There is nothing you can do to make Him not love you. There's nothing you can do to earn your way to Him. He chose you, and when you accept Him in your heart and choose to follow Him, you don't have to worry about a thing. Truly. Because He won every battle already, he helps us be virtuous. He helps us be like Him. So, the pressure is off. If you want to invite Jesus in your heart, I encourage you to pray this prayer:

Dear Jesus,

Thank you for loving me. Thank you for dying on the cross to save me from my sins. I choose to accept you into my heart. Forgive me of my sins. I choose to turn away from my past and to follow You. Thank you for never giving up on me. I believe you rose from the grave and are my Lord and my Savior.

In Jesus name I pray,

Amen.

If you prayed that prayer then I am so proud of you! Even more importantly, Heaven is rejoicing and they are partying, celebrating YOU, who once was lost but now you are found! I encourage you to get plugged into a local Bible believing church and find Christians in your hometown where they can help you and encourage you on this journey of faith. This is the best decision you will ever make in your life. Yay God!

Okay now let's resume.

Moving on to the next part of the verse, it says "She is far more precious than rubies." I want you to say out loud right now "FAR MORE!". You are far more precious than rubies. Fun fact: Rubies actually represent good fortune and courage, and God says you're worth far more than what rubies are worth. See, I believe God revealed something to me about rubies. Rubies are something of this Earth. Rubies are made under the earth from high temperatures and extreme pressure. For many years, a ruby seems to go "unnoticed", "hidden", "unseen" and not only that, it goes through a lot of intense heat and pressure in order to form into something beautiful. We generally don't see how rubies are formed, however, we tend to see the finished product. The beautiful, shiny, crystal gem. In some ways, perhaps we can relate to the ruby.

It reminds me of my past. My past is filled with moments where I have felt unnoticed, hidden and unseen. On top of that, I have also gone through depression, anxiety, trauma, pain and suffering. Yet, I am alive today. I'm not only surviving, but thriving. All because through the dark times, God was with me. Not only was He with me, He was taking my past and creating it into something beautiful. Today I can say my life is beautiful. Not because it is perfect, but because I serve a perfect God who cares about my imperfections. So since a ruby goes through a hard process and yet comes out beautiful and is one of the most sought after stones here on earth, God says you are worth FAR MORE than rubies. Rubies are sought after because people saw the end product. But you have been sought after from the beginning of time, even before you messed up. Even when God knew you were going to mess up, He still sought after you. See, because rubies have value, they cost a high price in order to own one. When God sees you and I, He recognizes our value and understood the price it cost to pay for our sins and for us to become His children. That is why God had to send His one and only son Jesus Christ to come to earth and die on a cross because that's the highest price that had to be paid to own us. Nothing else would suffice. 1 Corinthians 6:20 says we are bought with a price. We belong to God.

"God bought you with a high price. So you must honor God with your body." 1 Corinthians 6:20 (NLT).

This verse was written before we were born. God spoke it before we were born, therefore; our worth was defined before we even came into this world. He saw your worth and He was willing to pay the high price because he loves you that much. God wants you to know how loved you are. You are worth FAR MORE than rubies to Him. I want to share Psalm 139:14-18 with you so that you can get a small glimpse as to how God feels about when you were created.

"I praise you because I am fearfully and wonderfully made; your works are wonderful, I know that full well. My frame was not hidden from you when I was made in the secret place, when I was woven together in the depths of the earth. Your eyes saw my unformed body; all the days ordained for me were written in your book before one of them came to be. How precious to me are your thoughts, God! How vast is the sum of them! Were I to count them, they would outnumber the grain of sand—when I awake, I am still with you." (NIV)

When God says we are fearfully made, it means we were made exceptionally well, remarkably, awfully, exceedingly and extremely well. When I think about this, it points to virtuous. God already made us virtuous from before we were even born. He already did it. He created us, from our most personal, inmost, truest self to the very exterior end of our fingernails and he calls us fearfully and wonderfully made. It is evident from just our very existence.

I want to share a personal story with you because I did not believe this for many years. I struggled with insecurity for most of my childhood and teenage years. I felt insecure about my physical appearance and about my personality. I was labeled shy and quiet, and yet it never sat right with me because deep down I knew that was not me. I had just allowed the enemy to silence me after feeling so abandoned by my dad when my parents divorced and I was a young child. Interestingly enough, I knew the woman that God called me to be. It was like I could see her from a distance, yet I didn't know if I would be able to attain that version of myself. Yet, in hindsight, I recognize that it's not about striving but about trusting God daily and just keeping my eyes on Him (in every detail of my life, not just the future ahead). One day, as I was walking to school, I felt that Jesus was walking with me. I felt like He was holding my hand, so I made a fist as if to hold His hand on the way to school. We talked. He showed me an image and it was of a little boy who drew a picture for his dad. He was so proud and excited to show his dad, and once his dad saw it, he said, "Wow! What a masterpiece!". Then Jesus reminded me that that is what God thinks of us. A masterpiece that HE created. He is so proud of you and me. And that's the beautiful thing about our Creator, if God had one definition of beautiful, we would all look the same. But we don't and we are ALL beautiful because we are ALL made in His image. His image clearly comes in all different shapes, colours and sizes and yet the bible says we are His masterpiece. WE. All of us. You. Me. So it must break God's heart when we don't like ourselves, or when we dislike our bodies or our skin tone. He says I made you. Fearfully and wonderfully. Imagine you creating something and the very thing you created doesn't even like itself. Or for the mothers reading this, imagine your own child not liking the way they are, which can be heartbreaking for the mother because they came out of you. You played a crucial role in bringing them to earth, and I'm sure you think they are the most beautiful and amazing creations in the world. It breaks God's heart when we don't love ourselves. If were not satisfied with who we are, we won't be satisfied with anything else that comes into our lives.

So, when Jesus revealed that image to me, it completely changed my perspective. I learned to love the way God created me.

We are so precious to God. We are worth far beyond rubies which is why Jesus had to die for us. The price was death.

John 3:16 says, *"For God so loved the world (you), that he gave his only Son, that whoever believes in him should not perish but have eternal life."(NIV)*

God did whatever he needed to do so that we could live with Him forever. He is that crazy about you.

Romans 5:8 says, *"But God shows his love for us in that while we were still sinners, Christ died for us." (ESV)*

God loved us even in our mess. Even when we didn't know Him yet, He saw us, chose us and loved us. What a beautiful love story. Again, He is crazy about you.

Galatians 2:20 says, *"My old self has been crucified with Christ. It is no longer I who live, but Christ lives in me. So I live in this earthly body by trusting in the Son of God, who loved me and gave himself for me." (NLT)*

This verse summarizes how I moved forward. How I continue to keep moving forward because it causes me to remember that when I chose Jesus Christ, to follow Him for the rest of my life and to live for him, the person I was that I perhaps didn't even like too much didn't matter. The second I gave my life to Jesus, she was gone. All the negative thoughts, hurts, pain, and struggles were gone. This is because she had to die so Christ can live through her. Hence again why I don't need to strive. She's already been attained because Jesus is already in me! And, His Spirit continues to show my flesh everyday what it looks like to be like Christ. It's not stressful, it's the grace of God. I just have to trust Him. And, so do you. When you give your life to Christ, you have his virtues, which makes you a virtuous woman. It's already inside of you. We are strong and courageous because Jesus IN us is strong and courageous.

I'd like to pray for you.

Dear Jesus,

Thank you for the cross. Because on the cross you took away our shame, our guilt, our iniquities, our pain. In exchange for you. Your virtues, your truth, your love and life. I pray for every single person reading this book right now. Speak to them. Touch them. Breathe on them. May they receive the truth about who you have said that they are. May it penetrate deep into their hearts. I believe you love them so much and are comforting them right now. Help them to let go of the past and to walk in this new identity that they have in You. Just by trusting in You. In the mighty name of Jesus I pray. Amen. So be it.

CHAPTER 2

Proverbs 31:11-12

"Her husband has full confidence in her and lacks nothing of value. She brings him good, not harm, all the days of her life."(NIV)

The NLT version of this scripture also says, *"her husband can trust her, and she will greatly enrich his life."* I love looking at the different versions of scripture because not only does it help you understand better but it also just emphasizes certain ideas that the author is saying. What stood out to me right away is that it is the woman that brings the man good. It is the woman who greatly enriches his life. This is focusing on what the woman can do for the man. It does not say anything about what the man can do for the woman. Sometimes I can't help but wonder if we've got it backwards in today's day and age. I often hear a lot of "what he can do for me" and "he gives me" "me, me, me". Yes, I believe men also can bring so much good to women but how we can serve others is the mind of Christ. How we can serve others is what Jesus is looking for. Christ came down to do one thing: serve. Matthew 20:28 says this,

"for even the Son of Man came not to be served but to serve others and to give his life as a ransom for many." (NIV)

If Jesus Christ, God's one and only son came down from heaven to earth to serve, then how much more do we ought to serve those around us. Yet, I can't help but think that we live in one of the most selfish generations known to man and I think it breaks the heart of God.

When we think about marriage today, some of the viewpoints that tend to be said according to my Google search are:

"I don't want to be tied down"

"I don't want to lose myself"

"my spouse needs to make me happy"

"my spouse must complete me"

"divorce is an easy option"

I have been married to my husband for 8 years now and I can easily say that these phrases are false. Marriage is what God intended from the beginning. And everything God intends is good. So that means marriage is good. We just need to understand from a godly perspective on what it looks like. It doesn't mean marriage is easy, but it is good. In other words, not all good things are easy.

To all the women reading this, whether you are single or married, please know, you don't have to lose who you are to be married. You can still be yourself. In fact, marriage actually helps you to be the best version of yourself. Why? Because it causes you to think of someone else other than yourself, and to think of that person often because you are married to them. You live with them, you do life with them. It causes you to humble yourself and love on somebody else despite their flaws. Not easy, but it is exactly what Jesus Christ has done for you and I. Perhaps you have heard of the phrase "marriage is not meant to make you happy, it's meant to make you holy". I believe this to be true. It does not mean that you can't be happy in marriage. You should be able to enjoy it the majority of the time! But the person you are married to is not supposed to make you happy. Only God can satisfy your deepest needs and through Him you will feel complete. This is true when you are single and remains true when/if you get married. Nobody else can do this for you because it is God's role.

When you are whole and fulfilled first, not looking for someone to complete you, but finding that wholeness in Jesus Christ, then you are able to have a healthy marriage. This is because then you don't have these high expectations from the other person. They will fail you. We are all human and humans will fail humans. God is the only one who cannot fail a human being. We will be hurt by our spouses, annoyed, angry, you name it. But that does not mean we give up. Jesus does not give up on us. It just directs us to rely on the Holy Spirit who gives us everything we need to love and be godly. 2 Peter 1:3 says it,

"His divine power has given us everything we need for a godly life through our knowledge of him who called us by his own glory and goodness." (NIV)

Before I met my husband, I had a list of what I "wanted" in a man. God had a different plan, as He usually does, and it's even better than what we think. But one thing He approved of that was at the top of my list, was that I put I want a man who loves God more than He loves me. I knew for myself that if I was going to get married, I needed to love God more than I loved my husband. In today's world that might sound crazy. But God should be our greatest love. And when He is, all of our other relationships will thrive. Because God is our foundation and He always leads us to love and to life. If my hope and faith was all put into my husband, he would disappoint me at some point and then I would be shattered. But my hope isn't in him it's in God, and when it's in God, He shows me how to love my husband unconditionally -through the good, the bad and the ugly, for better or for worse, and vice versa for my husband. Because we both had this priority, I can see how strong our marriage is now. Not because we don't have bumps along the way, but because at the end of the day, we both find our joy and wholeness which comes from Jesus Christ, and that is what keeps our marriage going.

So, going back to the part on enriching a man's life, as this proverbs 31 woman does to her husband, I believe we are an extension of man, made from the rib of Adam and because of that, we (women) were created to help men. In Genesis 2:18, God says,

"it is not good for the man to be alone. I will make a helper suitable for him." (NIV).

The woman, Eve, was literally created to keep the man, Adam company and to help him in life.

I know that no feminist probably wants to hear this. BUT, this does not mean that Eve was Adam's slave. They were partners, created to rule over the Earth together, to have an abundant and successful life together. But her role was also very much to help and serve him. This does not mean that Eve lost herself. Eve was still EVE. She still had her own thoughts, opinions, judgments and temptations, almost to a fault because the snake tempted Eve in the garden, to try to eat from the tree she was not supposed to eat from. Eve in her free will, chose (not ruled by Adam), to eat from it and sinned.

Eve was always just as valuable as her husband. God could not find a helper that was just right for Adam. None of the animals were good enough, so God literally took a rib from Adam to make another human being that was just right. Women are so valuable. They are just as valuable as men are. Both are breathed and created by God himself.

What's interesting about the beginning of the chapter in Proverbs 31:10 is that it starts off with the virtues and characteristics of the woman, then the marriage is brought up after. I don't think this is by accident. Her foundation is laid down first on her identity; who she is in Christ, as a daughter of the King. She knows who she is before the man. She knows *whose* she is before the man, which is so important when getting into any relationship and definitely marriage. In marriage there will be storms. When two imperfect people are making a covenant together, there will be misunderstandings, miscommunication, disagreements, etc. But that does not mean we have to be afraid when those things happen, or give up, or think we married the wrong person. As long as we are human, there will be trials. But thankfully, when we build our life on Jesus, He gives us everything we need to face those trials and be triumphant in them. It reminds me of the man who built his house on the rock.

Matthew 7:24-27 says this,

"Anyone who listens to my teaching and follows it is wise, like a person who builds a house on solid rock. Though the rain comes in torrents and the floodwaters rise and the winds beat against that house, it won't collapse because it is built on bedrock. But anyone who hears my teaching and doesn't obey it is foolish, like a person who builds a house on sand. When the rains and floods come and the winds beat against that house, it will collapse with a mighty crash." (NLT)

In these verses, Jesus is speaking and saying how it is inevitable that rain and floodwaters and winds WILL come. It is not a matter of if, but when. And when they do, the only thing that can keep us standing is the word of God. Not just listening to it but actually doing it.

It is harder to humble yourself and forgive rather than to put up walls and push people away. It is harder to be slow to anger and turn the other cheek rather than cuss someone out. It's harder to search ourselves rather than be critical of someone else. These things are hard! That is why Jesus sent us the most precious and valuable gift, the Holy Spirit. Because it is only by the Holy Spirit that we are able to do these things.

Maybe you are reading this and feeling like you missed your chance in a relationship because your hurt, pain or insecurities caused you to push away or blame someone else. God knows your pain. He knows the crap you experienced. It was awful. Brutal. You did not deserve that. Please hear me. Whatever pain you're carrying, Jesus wants you to give it to Him. He wants to redeem and restore you. But, there are certain things we need to let go of so that He can enter in. When we have unforgiveness in our hearts, bitterness, pride etc. It's not that God does not want to help us, it's just that he literally cannot enter that area of our lives until we fully surrender to Him. That means listening and obeying. As hard as that may seem. I have been there. It's extremely tough. But the power of the Holy Spirit is tougher. The word of God is sharper. Keep going sis. Keep the faith and trust in the living God. Your breakthrough is coming.

Chapter 3

Proverbs 31:13-19

*"She finds wool and flax and busily spins it.
She is like a merchant's ship, bringing her food from afar.
She gets up before dawn to prepare breakfast for her household and plan the day's work for her servant girls. She goes to inspect a field and buys it; with her earnings she plants a vineyard. She is energetic and strong, a hard worker. She makes sure her dealings are profitable; her lamp burns late into the night. Her hands are busy spinning thread, her fingers twisting fiber."* NLT

Wow. If you are like me when reading this, you're probably like okaaayyyy good job! Congratulations. You win woman of the next 20 years award! I mean, when I read this I was like this woman seriously does it all, and I am slacking BIG time. But as I continued to read it, I first recognized God saying to me these things:
1.) not to compare.
2.) learn from her.
It's not about how much you can do. I find that these days our world is focused on how hard you work and if you work yourself into the ground it's considered honorable. Yes, we need to work in this life. Yes, hard work is good. But God never meant for us to work so hard that we don't have time for anything or anyone else. Or to work so hard that we make ourselves overwhelmed and sick. As I continued to study this passage, I realized that this woman is really great at being productive. Yes, she has a full day. It appears that pretty much every minute of her day could be accounted for. She really maximizes her day, and that was eye opening for me. It's not that she does more, she just uses her time really well and has learned to organize and prioritize.

Let's start at the beginning of the passage in verse 13. It says she finds wool and flax. It's as if she discovers or realizes what has been made available to her and activates her skill. It's an opportunity. And so she became productive with what she had. She started spinning. Started creating something. This woman recognizes an ability that she has and uses it! I believe we have all been given abilities. We also have all been given gifts according to 1 Peter 4:10-11.

This woman had the ability to create something useful and practical which could be used as a gift to help others. Sometimes I think we have gifts and abilities that lie dormant because we choose not to activate them. I want to challenge you in this moment to stop and think about the abilities and giftings God has given you. Are you using them? I believe we will be the most fulfilled when we are using our gifts and abilities to the glory of God. Why? Because I believe it is how we are wired. We can do what we do because of how God created us. When we fan into flame our gifts and abilities we are walking out life in the way God uniquely created us to be. Therefore, we are satisfied when we are doing what God created us to do, all for His glory.

The next verse says she is like a merchant's ship… let's just stop right there. What an interesting comparison for a woman! I have never heard a woman being compared to a merchant's ship, but here we are. I went ahead and looked up a merchant's ship. They are quite large boats (this does not help with the comparison) and they are also considered vessels. These ships transport cargo or they can carry passengers. In contrast to a pleasure craft which is used for pleasure and is recreational, this woman is like a merchant ship. She is a vessel. Used for great purposes and works hard to provide for those around her. In order to do this, this woman has to be strong. She must be physically and mentally strong because it is a lot of work and requires no hint of laziness. I believe this requires determination and having a deep understanding of her purpose in life. Let's keep reading.

The passage continues to say that she get's up before dawn! This woman has things to do. She has a lot of responsibility and in order to try to ensure everything goes smoothly, she is wise to get up before everyone else and plan the day and prepare breakfast. I don't know about you, but I love the feeling of being "ahead of the game". I love being "on top of things" because it's less stress. Some of us are stressed because we sleep too much and are not planning and preparing ahead of time. I am guilty of this. And it's not to condemn us but just a reminder to try a new perspective and to see that maybe some of the stress in our lives could be alleviated by getting up earlier and planning and preparing our day.

My husband is actually reading a book called the 5am club. I would make fun of him because I'm like, "Are you seriously going to get up at 5am?" "Who get's up at 5am? Willingly!?" But he went on to tell me that some of the most successful people in the world wake up at 5am. I also recognized that the Bible mentions waking up early to seek the Lord. Mark 1:35 says this,

"Before daybreak the next morning, Jesus got up and went out to an isolated place to pray." NLT

There are benefits to waking up early. Especially to seek God. Jesus had a lot on his plate. He needed to get up early and get his mind right. He had a responsibility. If He didn't have much responsibility, it would probably be a lot easier for Him to sleep in until midday. But Jesus was on assignment. He had a mission to complete. So in order to maximize His day, in order to not be overcome by stress and anxiety, He got up early when it was quiet to meet with His Father.

So my husband started getting up at 5am and he has seen a drastic change in his life. It's not easy at the start, but it encourages me to see him feel much more productive in his day and create structure. I always feel better when I get up early and get a good start to my day. I hope this encourages you to try the same if you haven't already.

Not only does this woman create clothing, she is in charge of her servants and household, and she also is a business woman! Can somebody say BOSS. BABE. Verse 16 says, *"she goes to inspect a field and buys it; with her earnings she plants a vineyard."* This virtuous woman makes her own income. I know these days everyone tends to make their own income, but back in the Bible days, not all the women had their own businesses and were investing. She took it upon herself to go above and beyond for her household. She has a well respected husband who I am assuming was able to provide for her and her family. But this woman wanted to do this for herself. I admire her because she educated herself and decided that she could bring something to the table alongside her husband in making income for her family. This is not to say that women who don't work or don't bring income are wrong. There are a variety of reasons for that. But what I do see from this is that she found a way to bring something to the table in her partnership with her husband and it benefits their life. I don't think a man would ever not appreciate a woman finding a way to enhance the life and quality of the home. Also for the woman, it is satisfying knowing that you can do something/create something on your own.

The adjectives to describe this woman are "energetic, strong and a hard-worker". This shows me that she is productive and she understands her purpose. I believe that when we are walking in the call God has for us, when we realize our responsibility that God has required for us to do on the earth and when we accept it, it helps us to be energetic, stay strong and work hard because we have vision and understanding of why we are here. This woman has so much strength for all the responsibilities God gave her. Not because she does not ever feel weak, but because her eyes stay fixed on Jesus.

In Jesus, we discover our purpose and the gifts God has given us which can be used for His glory. When we are fully walking this out, we are the most satisfied and the most fulfilled because we have each been placed on this earth for a reason.

The last verse we will look at for this chapter says, *"her hands are busy spinning thread, her fingers twisting fiber."*

Like I have said before, this woman is very productive. There does not seem to be an hour in the day that is not accounted for. She maximizes her day from morning to night. She's busy, but busy in a good way. It is good to be focused. It is good to be occupied so that you don't fall into temptation doing something else or doing nothing at all. The bible says this,

"Lazy hands make for poverty, but diligent hands bring wealth." Proverbs 10:4 (NIV)

It can be hard at times to be productive or feel productive. To me, sometimes it seems tedious, or to be honest, I just feel too tired. It is definitely important to rest. But there is a difference between laziness and rest. A lot of the time, being productive is doing things we don't want to do. I don't think this woman always wanted to do everything listed in this chapter. But I do think she had good discipline, focus and responsibility that drove her to continue what she was doing. If I can be super open and vulnerable with you, sometimes it is hard for me to find the time or the desire to write this book. It's not that I don't want to, I see the end goal, I see the vision for this book, but when reality hits and it's been an exhausting day with the kids, I feel like sitting down, grabbing a snack and watching TV. Which again, rest is good. But, if I'm doing that night after night and neglecting the idea that I believe God gave me to write this book, then that would be laziness. Nobody said being productive was easy, but it's always worth it.

As women, I believe we are meant to be productive. God did not make us just to stand around and look pretty. We have a purpose in life just as much as men have a purpose in life. In Genesis 2:18, the Bible talks about God saying man shouldn't be alone and that God will give the man a helper that is just right for the man.

We are supposed to be a TEAM with men. We are supposed to be a team with our husbands. Adam was working and tending to the garden, but he still needed a helper. When Adam saw his wife, he said, "At last!" or some versions say "Finally!". He was relieved! It was what he needed. We may have different gifts, but it always works best when we work together.

As we end this section of the Proverbs 31 woman, here are a couple questions for you to reflect on:

1.) What are your giftings?

2.)   What can you do to be more productive in your day? (this doesn't necessarily mean more busy, but more productive)

Chapter 4

Proverbs 31:20

"She extends a helping hand to the poor and opens her arms to the needy."
(NLT)

Two actions I notice right away in this verse is that this woman extends and what she opens. Let's start with extends. By extending towards something or someone is initiating something. She has made a decision to help, to offer, to hold out. It is making a choice to do something without knowing the outcome.

Extending doesn't necessarily mean you will receive something back, but this woman made a decision to help regardless of what will happen next. To me that shows strength, courage and even vulnerability. The purpose of reaching out to others is to help, encourage and uplift one another without expecting anything in return.

So she extends a helping hand to the poor. The poor are people who need help. The poor is someone who you can see is lacking or deficient in something (generally with money) and they need something that you have. The Proverbs 31 woman knew what she had, and we all know as well after going through everything she does on a daily basis, and yet instead of hoarding her earnings, she decides to give. It enables her to sow. Luke 6:38 says this:

"Give, and it will be given to you. A good measure, pressed down, shaken together and running over, will be poured into your lap. For with the measure you use, it will be measured to you."(NIV)

That verse in Luke is a principle in the bible. It is how things work, however, verse 20 in Proverbs 31 tells me that this woman was not giving just to receive. Because it continues on to say "she opens her arms to the needy". It is one thing to give. It is one thing to help someone out and do a good deed. It is another thing to open up yourself and allow someone in, in order to help him/her on a deeper level. To open up your arms indicates that you are allowing someone to have access to you. You're not closed off or have a wall up. She invites those who need her, people who depend on her. It permits vulnerability, and I believe it is also a sign of strength. When we let someone in need in, we can truly be helpful not just on a physical level of supplying needs, but on an emotional, mental and spiritual level as well.

I recently spoke at a women's event at my church on the topic of multigenerational sisterhood and why that is so important in the kingdom of God. My mentor and I look nothing alike, we come from different backgrounds, we are different ages, and yet when she decided to open up her arms to me and allow me to fully be in her life, well, it completely changed my life. By opening up her arms and opening up herself to me, she was able to help me, who was in dire need of healing.

The Proverbs 31 woman in this passage displays selflessness which tends to be completely opposite of our generation today. I am not saying this generation can't be selfless, but when it comes to social media, a lot of it is geared towards self and letting others look at you and letting them into the highlight reel of your life and not the whole reel of your life. Highlight reels are awesome and we can celebrate the high points of people's lives. But we have to be careful if that is all we see because then we start to look inward and may feel like our life needs to only be a highlight reel. Jesus says in John 16:33, "in this world you will have trouble. But take heart! I have overcome the world." The Proverbs 31 woman is an amazing woman but not a perfect woman, and yet with her life that appears well accomplished, she still recognizes that this world is not just about her but about the lives of so many others as well.

A Proverbs 31 woman sows and reaps, and we all have something we can sow. She meets physical needs like Jesus did when he sent manna from heaven so the Israelites could survive, and He also healed a lame man. But Jesus didn't just heal the lame man, He also forgave him. Jesus was able to meet a physical and a spiritual need. The Proverbs 31 woman is able to meet physical needs but because she is also a daughter of the King, she is able to meet spiritual needs as well.

I can't help but wonder why the next verse would say "she has no fear of winter for her household, for everyone has warm clothes." I believe every word is placed in the Bible for a specific reason and purpose. We just read how the Proverbs 31 woman extends her hands to the poor and helps the needy, yet, she has no fear of winter and everyone in her family is covered? Could it be that when we focus on serving others, God will provide for our needs? We can have a confident faith and hope just like this Proverbs 31 woman, that when we are walking in the will of God, He will come through for us.

When I was studying this verse (Proverbs 31:20), God really spoke to me about social media. You might be wondering, how on earth does this relate to social media? I will gladly explain it to you! As I said earlier, this generation is a social media generation. When we are too focused on self, we are unable to see the needs of others and the opportunities around us to actively reach out and sow.

So God specifically told me, if I go on social media, it needs to be for a purpose. Too often I have been on social media just aimlessly scrolling. It wastes so much of my time! Precious time that we have here on earth. So God told me, if you're going to be on social media, SOW. If I am not intentional about why I am on social media, it can and will consume some part of me and will distract me of my time, emotions and purpose.

What I mean by sowing, is that whenever I am on social media, I try to be intentional. I am intentional to compliment someone or to congratulate someone or even just to actually like their post if that's how I truly feel and not just scroll by it pretending I didn't see it. It is to celebrate others and sow words of encouragement, love and truth into those that I follow. This will help me to walk in the fruit of the Spirit and also not to spiral down a path that makes me feel ungrateful for my life, or leads me to depression because I started comparing myself. I haven't been perfect at it, but when I remember to be intentional, it changes the way I view and interact with social media.

Is social media bad?

It can be so easy to be drenched in the social media world. For me personally, I have struggled (and still do sometimes) with always making sure I have my phone on me and not with the thought in mind for emergencies but with the thought that if I don't have my phone on me, I might miss something, "something" really important on my social media feed. It became subconscious. I didn't fully realize at the time that that's why I felt the need to have my phone on me. But in hindsight, I see that for me, that truly was the reason. I needed to keep myself "updated" on what was going on in the world... the world of social media. See, I never cared for the news. I was never bent on feeling I needed to keep up with the news, and since it felt so negative to me, I would rather not look at it...and was confident that I would hear of major incidents through others. But with social media, that was something I felt I needed to be updated on. It wasn't even that I enjoyed it all the time either, but it became something I depended on. An idol. I would take my phone and automatically open up Facebook or Instagram and just start to scroll aimlessly without any real purpose to it. I would spend lots of valuable time doing that. Looking back, I can see how this could have contributed to my symptoms of anxiety and depression. There are a lot of voices on social media, and not all of them are positive or good for our soul. So I was not being purposeful about what I fed my soul. I was feeding my soul whatever it saw, as it came. Jesus says that *"Your eye is like a lamp that provides light for your body. When your eye is healthy, your whole body is filled with light. But when your eye is unhealthy, your whole body is filled with darkness. And if the light you think you have is actually darkness, how deep that darkness is!" (Matthew 6:22-23). NIV*

Since I was not carefully taking care of my soul by being cautious about what my eyes see, there were some negative effects that came into my life because of that. All this to say, I am not saying that social media is bad. I think there is and can be a great purpose and use for it, if it is used the right way. James 1:17 in the Message version says, *"So my very dear friends, don't get thrown off course. Every desirable and beneficial gift comes out of heaven. The gifts are rivers of light cascading down from the Father of Light. There is nothing deceitful in God, nothing two-faced, nothing fickle. He brought us to life using the true Word, showing us off as the crown of all his creatures."*

In reading that scripture, I believe that everything good and beneficial is meant to bring life not death. I believe it is meant to bring about good and give more glory to God. With the proper use of social media, it can and has done wonders by spreading the Good News to people all over the world. Through social media we can now connect with others on a global scale, worship together, hear the Word together and so much more. With its proper use, it is meant to bring so much life.

So why do we sometimes feel depressed, anxious, etc. after being on social media? Why do we sometimes need to take a social media fast? Well, social media can be distracting and subtly begin to weigh us down. Depending on what we are looking at, it can take our minds off the things of heaven and start to get caught up in earthly things. Social media, simply put, has been tainted. It is a God idea but the enemy took a good idea and a God idea and twisted it. So now, the devil can use social media to his benefit, to try to get people to compare themselves and have them feeling weighed down, with low self-esteem and a desire to achieve earthly rewards, not Godly rewards.

But…. The enemy has already been defeated! God is calling His children to take back what belongs to God. I believe God is calling His children to invade social media, to invade the walls of comparison, to invade the walls of insecurity, to invade the walls of insignificance and instead, to be bold. To be strong and courageous just as he commanded Joshua. God wants us to use our voice as Christians and stand for His word - even on social media. He's watching. The Bible says in Proverbs 5:21, "For the Lord sees clearly what a man does, examining every path he takes" NLT. The Lord sees when we are silent. He sees when we have an opportunity to speak up and he sees how we steward the resources He gives us. Social media is an opportunity for us to be a light and an encouragement of God's work and to speak the name of Jesus. Not just for selfies and stories of food. It's an opportunity. I'm not saying those things are bad, but I encourage you to pray and ask God what He wants you to use your social media for that day. Maybe there's a verse He wants you to share or a sermon that touched your heart that others need to hear. I encourage you to share Jesus through the vehicle of social media.

So really to sum it ALL up, this is what I am saying; be the change. A Proverbs 31 woman sows and reaps. So let's sow! I encourage you to see social media as a way to sow into the lives of others. Comment, like and encourage. Let's do it together and invade the negative walls of social media and bring the kingdom of God to the whole world.

Chapter 5

Proverbs 31:21

"She has no fear of winter for her household, for everyone has warm clothes" (NLT)

I love when I read that a woman has no fear. Especially a mother. And especially when she is in a situation where it is understandable to have a bit of fear. See, I am a mother myself and I must say, I don't think I have ever experienced more fear and anxiety in my life until I became a mom. It is definitely much better now, but when I first became a mom, my mama bear instincts were in full mama bear mode. I didn't really want anyone touching my baby, watching my baby, let alone breathe on my baby! I was very protective, and I believe I always will be. Now, some of that is natural. I believe it is the way God created women and especially mothers to be. We should protect our kids, we should be cautious, we should want them to be safe. But there's a difference between being protective and being paranoid which can also be seen as being overly protective. The definition of paranoid, according to Google, is being "unreasonably or obsessively anxious, suspicious or mistrustful." I think in the beginning I was riding a fine line between the two. Sometimes I was overly cautious or obsessively anxious because of fear. Fear was the driving factor for me at times when perhaps I was being a bit unreasonable.

What I love about the Proverbs 31 woman is that she has no fear and not just no fear, no fear of winter for her entire household.

Now in this text, I automatically think of the season of winter especially since it follows with, "for everyone has warm clothes". Everyone is taken care of. This is a season where you might be extra cautious, wanting to make sure your family is safe, healthy and warm. But she is not fearful. She is not fearful of this "difficult" season.

I believe the proof of having a peace that surpasses all understanding, a peace that comes in every situation no matter the circumstance, is a peace that comes from the only one who is peace Himself and that is Jesus Christ, and having that peace in the hard seasons of your life. That's when you know you truly have the peace of God.
The Bible says this in 2 Thessalonians 3:16,

"Now may the Lord of peace himself give you his peace at all times and in every situation. The Lord be with you all." NLT.

We might be thinking of the season of winter when reading this text but I also think of seasons of winter emotionally, spiritually, mentally and physically. The thing about the Proverbs 31 woman is that she knew winter was coming. She knew the season had to come. So because she knew winter was coming, she was prepared for it. She was ready, therefore, she had no fear. She got ahead of the season. She prepared in advance so that her family and everyone in her household could be safe. I think that sometimes we forget that winter is coming. Sometimes we forget that we go through seasons, we go through changes and that these changes have to happen in order for us to grow in our faith. As long as we are on the earth, we will go through seasons. We don't know when each season will come, but it is good to be prepared as best as we can spiritually. In the Bible, Ephesians chapter 6 talks about being prepared spiritually so that we can stand firm against the devil's schemes. Somehow our world tries to make us think that you can live a life without any trouble or tribulation here on earth. But that is not the case. James 1:2-4 says

"Consider it pure joy, my brothers and sisters, whenever you face trials of many kinds, because you know that the testing of your faith produces perseverance. Let perseverance finish it's work so that you may be mature and complete, not lacking anything." NIV

I hate to burst anyone's bubble, but it's not a matter of if but when. And because we know this, we can prepare for it the best we can by staying close to Jesus.

I think of the Bible and the story in Matthew 14 of the disciples who just came out of an amazing season. Jesus and the disciples fed five thousand with only five loaves of bread and two fish, a season of miracles! Then basically immediately after that, the disciples got into a boat to travel and got hit with a storm and became afraid. Jesus started walking on water towards them and the disciples freaked out. They did not recognize Jesus in their fear. They thought He was a ghost. One of the disciples, Peter, said to Jesus, "Lord, if it's really you, tell me to come to you, walking on water." Jesus told Peter to come, but as the environment around him got worse (the wind and the waves), Peter freaked out and started crying out to Jesus for help. Jesus saved him right away, but he questioned why Peter's faith was so small and why they doubted him. I think He questioned them especially after they just participated in helping Jesus do an amazing miracle! Fear can easily and quickly cloud our judgment of the truth. The truth was that they were safe. Why? Because Jesus was there. They did not feel safe because of their environment, and let their environment distract them from focusing on the truth. Another interesting part I noticed was that Jesus was coming to them on water, performing another miracle, after just finishing praying to God. Jesus' faith was built up, therefore another miracle happened. The disciples did not pray (at least it wasn't mentioned anyway), therefore when the next season hit, instead of believing for the miracle, they allowed their emotions to lead them astray. They forgot that winter was coming. They also forgot that the one who was with them in the sunny season was also the same one with them in the storm. This is why we must constantly stay connected to the source. Because in this world, it is so easy to get distracted by anything other than Jesus. This specifically is a message for believers because this is Jesus who we walk with daily and yet we still can forget that He is with us always.

I also believe that because the Proverbs 31 woman in the previous verse was so busy taking care of the needs of others, when she could have been taking care of the needs of her own family, especially knowing that winter is coming, perhaps she could have been making extra clothes etc. But instead, she decides to help the poor and needy. God watches that and blesses her with provision and protection in the next season, winter.

My question for you is, do you believe everything will be okay? The Proverbs 31 woman had no fear and that means she had peace. She had faith to believe and know that no matter what comes, everything was covered. Winter has to come. Jesus had to die. Not everything is pleasant, but in the end it can be beneficial. We cannot go through life without hardships. It's because of hardships that we appreciate beautiful moments. And God is so kind that despite the hardships, He promises that He is with us, always. Do you believe that?

Matthew 28:18-20 says this,

"Then Jesus came to them and said, "All authority in heaven and on earth has been given to me. Therefore go and make disciples of all nations, baptizing them in the name of the Father and of the Son and of the Holy Spirit, and teaching them to obey everything I have commanded you. And surely I am with you always, to the very end of the age."NIV

That verse is our hope as believers. That despite trials, we are on a mission in this world and we are not in it alone. We can have a steadfast peace and faith when going through hardships because of Jesus Christ. Even Jesus had hardships, but now He wears the victor's crown, and overwhelming victory is ours.

Chapter 6

Proverbs 31:22-24

"She makes her own bedspreads. She dresses in fine linen and purple gowns. Her husband is well known at the city gates, where he sits with the other civic leaders. She makes belted linen garments and sashes to sell to the merchants." NLT

This Proverbs 31 woman never ceases to amaze me. I mean, now she's making her own bedspreads! I admire this about her because it goes to show the discipline and the desire she has to create her own things and not be lazy. She takes responsibility and ensures that she is able to make what she needs to and because she can. I can see through these scriptures that this woman values herself and what God has given her. She uses her own resources and stewards well, what God has entrusted her with.

She dresses in fine linen and purple gowns. Revelation 19:7-8 says,

"Let us rejoice and be glad and give him glory! For the wedding of the Lamb has come, and his bride has made herself ready. Fine linen, bright and clean, was given her to wear." (Fine linen stands for the righteous acts of God's holy people). NIV

So this woman chooses to dress herself in what represents as righteous and pure. To be honest, it's hard for me to truly define righteousness. But the way I see it is being good in the eyes of God. God is righteous, the ultimate level of excellence and in right standing. We are able to be seen as that to God because of his Son, Jesus Christ. The Proverbs 31 woman chooses to be dressed in fine linen. She chooses to represent herself as righteous. I think how we view ourselves represents the way we display ourselves, including how we dress. What we choose to show others outwardly, can display how we feel internally but it could also hide how we feel internally. But I believe that this woman was honest inside and out and demonstrated the way she dressed as how she felt internally because of her relationship with God.

I used to struggle with choosing what I wore. Especially when it came to church. At times, I kept wondering if the outfits I was picking were appropriate enough or dressy enough. From time to time I don't mind dressing up but I generally love looking cute yet having a style that is comfy and casual. Also, a lot of what is selling in stores can be quite revealing and yet it was in-style, and I wanted to fit in with the trends. But as I have grown up, I recognized I had to draw the line somewhere. What I wear represents God. If I call myself a believer, I want to represent Him well in every single area of my life, including clothes! This doesn't mean God is boring and I can't have fun with it or that I have to make sure I am covered up from head to toe. I believe God cares about every little thing in our lives including what we wear. I actually feel more free knowing that God cares and that I represent Him. I get to choose what I wear and show others that being a Christian is not boring. I can express myself through clothing in whatever style I want!!! I may decide to wear mom jeans and beanie one day, or a bucket hat with a neon sweater the next day. Why? Because God is creative and He is expressive. He expresses Himself through creation. Look at all the colours in the sunset, look at all the animals he has made and the mountains and human beings! He made us all in HIS image, how expressive is our God! He is expressed in multiple ways. He's a designer and He cares about everything we do. Because He cared from the very beginning. He cared what Adam and Eve wore. Genesis 3:21 says,

"And the Lord God made clothing from animal skins for Adam and his wife." NLT

To give some context to this verse, see, in the beginning, Adam and Eve were created and they were both naked. They didn't have any shame about it, until the serpent came to them and convinced Eve that she could disobey God and eat fruit from a tree she was not supposed to eat from. He convinced Eve to eat the forbidden fruit and she shared it with her husband, Adam. Once they disobeyed, they realized good and evil and immediately felt shame because they were naked. So they made clothes out of fig leaves to cover themselves. God then starts looking for them and once He finds them, they explain what happened and how they disobeyed. There were consequences for them and the serpent. But God also covers them with His grace. He does this by saying *"He will strike your head, and you will strike his heel."* Genesis 3:15, giving them victory over the enemy. But also, God made them clothes from animal skin and physically covered them. Now, Adam and Eve already had coverings. They made their own clothes from leaves. Yet even despite their disobedience, God loved them so much, that He covered them with something even better than what they could do on their own. Therefore, also making God the first fashion designer!

See, God cares, even about what we wear! Yes, we make mistakes but He wants to get right in there with us and help us and cover us from our past and comfort us. He doesn't want us to stay in our shame. Does He agree with sin? Absolutely not. But when we admit our sin and allow Him to help us, He covers us so beautifully and better than anything we could do on our own.

The Proverbs 31 woman also dresses in purple gowns. The color purple is a very prestigious color. In the Bible it is seen to represent royalty or majesty, as well as wealth, luxury and/or prosperity. This is what she dresses in. She is a daughter of the most high and she dresses like it. When we become believers, we are adopted in God's family as his sons and daughters. The Bible says,

"But you are a chosen people, a royal priesthood, a holy nation, God's special possession, that you may declare the praises of him who called you out of darkness in his wonderful

light." 1 Peter 2:9. NIV

Other versions go on to say that we may proclaim the excellencies of him, or the virtues of him. The Proverbs 31 woman is a virtuous woman. She represents these virtues inside and out.

The scripture goes on to say that her husband is well known at the city gates and that he sits with the civic leaders. This shows me that her husband is in good standing with some top leaders in their community. As a result, the way the Proverbs 31 woman dresses and presents herself is a reflection of her husband. I believe that the Proverbs 31 woman is aware that the way she acts and dresses always reflects Jesus but then it also reflects her husband. A husband and wife are one. They become one flesh as it mentions to us in the book of Genesis. Therefore, when you are married, you represent not just yourself, but also your spouse, and I believe the Proverbs 31 woman and her husband do a great job of supporting and reflecting each other. The verse says that her husband sits with the other civic leaders. To sit with means to spend time with. I believe this also goes to show that the civic leaders respect her husband. He has good character by being well-known and respected enough to sit with the civic leaders. Because this man is so well respected, it is great that his wife also believes confidently in who she is as well and reflects herself and her husband in the same way, just through a different vehicle. This vehicle is by making her own belted linen garments and sashes to sell to the merchants. In this way, her own way, she is also becoming respected by her community through the work that she does while also gaining profit to contribute to her family.

I know we talked about this earlier on in the book, but I can't help but notice how much the Proverbs 31 passages talk about what the Proverbs 31 woman does and what she creates and how she contributes to the family. It is not to say that everybody has to do this. There is no comparison in how much a woman does. But I believe what God is trying to say is that it does not have to be "one" way, and it should not be "one way" when it comes to womanhood and motherhood. God gave women other desires and hopes and plans other than being a mom. He gave us the ability to birth what looks so tiny into something big and extraordinary. Yes that goes for children but it is not limited to it. He also gave us brains which are filled with ideas and visions and dreams and hopes and desires to give birth and grow into something amazing! Whether it's a business or creative arts or developing a skill, most of us have a desire for more. What we want to accomplish in life. This Proverbs 31 woman is an example to us saying that it is possible. It can be done. You can be a wife, a mother, and a business woman all in one without losing your mind! Jesus gives her the ability and capacity to do it. Do what is in your capacity. We are all different, and we all have different capacities. But maybe your capacity is larger than you think. Are you settling? Is there a desire you have that you've put on the back burner thinking it's just not possible? Does that desire still go through your mind? Does it burn within you and you just can't seem to shake it? God put it there for a reason. Because it is possible, with Him.

I just want to encourage someone reading this right now, that all things ARE possible with God. He doesn't want us to settle, He wants us to live life with abundance and be overflowing with joy and peace and love and that includes giving us the desire of our hearts as we delight in HIM. It's not too late. God works outside of time. 2 Peter 3:8 says,

"But do not forget this one thing, dear friends: With the Lord a day is like a thousand years, and a thousand years are like a day." NIV

I love how the verse starts off by saying, 'do not forget'. Because for many of us, it's so easy to forget that God is not like us. We think with human mentality. God's thoughts are not our thoughts, and His ways are not our ways. What could take us 1000 years, God can do in 1 day! Be encouraged, my dear sister, that God is able. He will do it. Trust in Him and let Him lead you and not your doubt.

Rediscovering You!

Chapter 7

Proverbs 31:25-26

"She is clothed with strength and dignity, and she laughs without fear of the future. When she speaks, her words are wise, and she gives instructions with kindness." NLT

Previously we talked about what the Proverbs 31 woman put on physically and how what she decided to wear portrayed a certain message. Now we are going to look at what she puts on mentally.

Verse 25 starts off by saying she is clothed. We all have a choice of what we decide to put on. The Proverbs 31 woman is choosing how she will see herself and what mindset she will approach life with. In this case, in her mental state, we can see that she has decided to put on strength. I believe that this is not a strength of her own but a divine strength that comes from her Heavenly Father.

The Bible says in Psalms 28:7-8 *"The Lord is my strength and my shield; my heart trusts in him, and he helps me. My heart leaps for joy, and with my song I praise him. The Lord is the strength of his people, a fortress of salvation for his anointed one."* NIV

Ephesians 6:10 says, *"Finally, be strong in the Lord and in his mighty power."* NIV

There are many verses that mention strength in the Bible, but I shared these two specifically because they really stood out to me. The first one from Proverbs clearly states that the Lord is our strength and shield and because the Proverbs 31 woman is a godly woman, her being clothed in strength is of the Lord himself. The verse also reveals that we don't need to be strong on our own. We have strength in our Lord, Jesus Christ and therefore, we don't have to muster up strength everyday when we wake up! Hallelujah! It can be super exhausting trying to be strong on our own. Ultimately, if we continue to be strong on our own, it will wear us down and perhaps we may feel even weaker than we did initially. But for the believer, the Lord is our strength, therefore, when we are weak, we are strong (2 Corinthians 12:10). You see I think we have to remember that this Proverbs 31 woman is not the "perfect" woman and that this image we have of her in the Bible is attainable, even in today's day and age. It just might present differently. It's not that she's perfect, it's that she is obedient to her Father.

The second verse I shared in Ephesians, says to "be strong in the Lord and in his mighty power." This is a command. So right away, it shows me that this Proverbs 31 woman is being obedient to what God's word says. She is not swayed by how she feels, she just decides to make a decision (an obedient decision) by doing what God's word says. We have a choice in how we choose to view ourselves and approach life. God will never force us to do anything, but Jesus does say in John 14:6, "I am the way, the truth and the life. No one can come to the Father except through me." So when we choose the way of Jesus and follow what His word says, we find a way to live life now here on earth that brings direction, truth and life to every area of our lives. Ultimately this brings us peace, joy and righteousness that we can experience now until we get to Heaven.

The verse also mentions that she is clothed in dignity. According to Google's dictionary, the definition of dignity is this: "the state or quality of being worthy of honor or respect." It can also mean self-respect or self-esteem. The Proverbs 31 woman chooses to believe what God says about her. Therefore, she has learned to love herself, respect herself and accept herself as being righteous, not because naturally she is righteous but because supernaturally through the blood of Jesus, she is a new creation and He has now made her righteous in His eyes. She chose to accept THAT truth and put it on.

A pastor once gave this illustration: he said that at big celebrity events, they don't ask you what are you wearing, they ask you, WHO are you wearing? The who represents prestige and status which can be more important than the actual article of clothing. The creator behind the article of clothing is what people care about.

We have a choice everyday to decide who we will wear. Will we put on the old self or will we put on the new self? This all starts within our minds. The Proverbs 31 woman is the way she is because of what she set her mind on.

Colossians 3:9-10 says, *"Do not lie to each other, since you have taken off your old self with it's practices and have put on the new self, which is being renewed in knowledge of it's Creator."* NIV

Colossians 3:2 says, *"Set your minds on things above, not on earthly things."* NIV

The Proverbs 31 woman's sights are set on the things of heaven. If it was set on the things of the earth (including ourselves, our flesh, etc.), she wouldn't be able to clothe herself in the things of heaven. When we clothe ourselves with these things, a peace comes from Jesus. I believe this is why the Proverbs 31 woman can laugh at the days to come without fear. It's because she has a sound mind. She has put on the mind of Christ.

One of my favourite verses is 2 Timothy 1:7 which says, *"For God has not given us a spirit of fear, but of power and of love and of a sound mind."* NKJV

The Bible also says in 1 Corinthians 2:16, *"For who has known the mind of the Lord that he may instruct Him? But we have the mind of Christ."* NKJV

God has given us the mind of Christ. This is so powerful when we are able to embrace and tap into it. The mental health issues in our world has skyrocketed and the struggle is within the human mind. Human minds get tired. Human minds get tainted. Human minds get affected by past traumas and childhood experiences. Human minds are weak. But now as believers, we are told we HAVE the mind of CHRIST. We no longer have the mind of a natural human being, we have the mind of a supernatural, all powerful, all wonderful, all loving, all-knowing GOD. With that automatically comes healing, peace, wisdom, understanding, and knowledge.

Therefore, because her mind is right, then what she speaks just naturally flows from what she has chosen to set her mind on. Out of her mouth flows wisdom and kindness. It's easier to speak with wisdom and kindness when that's what is in your heart. I have noticed the difference within myself when I try to create my own wisdom to appear wise compared to when I rely on God to give me wisdom, and it just flows out of my mouth. I have also noticed the difference when I am trying really hard to be kind, especially when I don't feel like being kind, but I know it's the right thing to do. It does not appear or feel genuine. Even if the other person recognizes it as genuine, I know internally it's not genuine. What I need in those moments is to pray and ask God to soften my heart, to change my heart, to help me love those who may be hard to love. It's a heart change that is needed.

The Bible says in Matthew 12:34,

"For out of the abundance of the heart the mouth speaks." NKJV

Our words are the fruit of our heart. Whatever comes out of our mouths reveal what is rooted within our heart. The Proverbs 31 woman is able to flow out words of wisdom and give instructions with kindness, not just because she is a good person, but because of who she spends time with and the environments she places herself in. I believe she is able to be known for speaking with wisdom and kindness because it became rooted within her. It was a part of her. I believe she spent quality time with her Heavenly Father, in order to be filled enough to speak His words of wisdom and kindness. It's important to recognize who we are surrounding ourselves with and what we are surrounding ourselves with. If we fill ourselves up with music that is degrading, cursing, and slandering others, that is what will flow out. If we are watching shows with inappropriate innuendos and suggestive language, then that is what will flow out.

I hope this will be an encouragement and a reminder for both you and I to be mindful of what we are allowing ourselves to be exposed to. As women of faith, I want to encourage you and challenge you to let go of that show you know you shouldn't be watching, or perhaps maybe it's a certain artist that isn't proclaiming the love of Christ. Maybe God is just wanting increased time with you, and there's an area of your life you haven't given to him. Whatever you let go of and give to God, He will fill. You'll see His amazing hand move in your life in a new and fresh way and you won't help but be able to proclaim His goodness, His kindness and love to others. Your heart will speak and act from a genuine place. Let's do this together, my sister. Let's be women of faith and rise up to all God has called us to be. Including in our speech.

Chapter 8

Proverbs 31:27-29:

"She carefully watches everything in her household and suffers nothing from laziness. Her children stand and bless her. Her husband praises her: There are many virtuous and capable women in the world, but you surpass them all!" NLT

I think one of the biggest rewards we can receive here on Earth is having our family honor us. The very people that we live life with, the people we raise, the person we grow old with, the people who see the good, the bad and the ugly! If they can stand and bless us, if our husband decides to praise us, then I really think that their approval or feedback is what matters most because they truly know us the best, and it tends to feel the most satisfying. Notice how this passage of scripture doesn't say "her friends" or "her boss"... well, kudos to this woman because she is her own boss! But it doesn't say "her employees", or "the church congregants". It says her family. I think that in life it is possible to have these other people in our lives bless us. It's possible to have overwhelming praises from our staff and boss at work. But, is it worth it if our family isn't pleased? I am learning more and more how much family is a blessing to me. It can be easy to take family for granted. But usually whenever we celebrate special moments such as birthdays or we graduate or we walk down the aisle, we generally want our family there. And, not just there, but in the first few rows if possible. Why? Because God created family to be our support system. Family was created so that we wouldn't have to do life alone. We have family because it teaches us at such a young age how to love, listen and respect one another, how to be kind, how to agree and disagree, how to create boundaries etc. All of this starts in the home, in our families. Unfortunately, there has been a ton of brokenness in families; there have been lots of unhealthy relationships and lots of trauma. That is not how God intended it to be. It's not that there needs to be a perfect family because nobody is perfect. However, God intended every family to be built off of a firm foundation which is Jesus. How do I know this? In the Bible, John 3:16 says,

"For God so loved the world that he gave is one and only Son, that whoever believes in him shall not perish but have eternal life."

So this verse says God SO loved us. He loved the world so much that He had to rescue us and let us live with Him forever in Heaven. We have all sinned and we have all fallen short of the glory of God (Romans 3:23), therefore God knew we were broken and ultimately headed towards death. But because He loves us so much, He sent Jesus, His Son, to rescue us from the grip of death by dying on the cross and being raised back to life. And, if we believe with our hearts and confess with our mouths that Jesus is Lord, we will be saved! (Romans 10:9). Therefore, we all have an opportunity to build healthy relationships, and Godly relationships because Jesus died that we might know Him. When we follow Jesus, we know Him. When we know Him, we desire to please Him.

So going back to this Proverbs 31 woman, it makes me smile and I feel encouraged that it is possible to raise children and to have a husband who gives us praises. Not because we are perfect but because we are following Jesus. Based on the verses we have read, we can say that this woman loved Jesus. Her life was centered around Him and it poured out into her family. It didn't come without hard work. She was the overseer of her household. She was carefully watching. The Bible says *"watch and pray so that you will not fall into temptation. The spirit is willing, but the flesh is weak."* (Matthew 26:41) NIV. Life can be extremely hard at times, we may feel like we want to let some things "slide" or not put in as much effort to do things the right way because it can get hard. We might want to numb ourselves by using other coping mechanisms. But, this woman was carefully watching over everything and she wasn't lazy. God was her strength. I thank God for being my strength. I think that could be what it is for this woman, like we mentioned in the previous chapter, it's not that she was always strong, it's that when she felt weak, God was strong.

Another thing to point out with this passage is that it says she *carefully* watches everything in her household. Some other words for carefully are: attentive, deliberately, faithfully, cautiously and correctly. This means she is invested. She is invested in what goes on at home. She oversees and makes sure everything is okay.

Just like God watches over us. The Bible says, *"The Lord is watching everywhere, keeping his eye on both the evil and the good."* Proverbs 15:3. NLT. God is invested in us. Have you ever binge watched a whole season of your favorite show because you really wanted to see what would happen next? Well, that's because you are invested. God is invested in us. He doesn't just want to watch though, He wants to help us walk through life with joy!

I also noticed that this woman watches over everything in her household specifically. It doesn't mention the fields she buys or the market that she sells her clothing items at. Her number one priority is her household. It's her first ministry. Your first ministry starts at home. I believe she reaped what she sowed because she made her children and her husband her first priority aside from Jesus.

I leave you then with these questions, what are you investing in? What is your first priority?

I encourage you to take some time to reflect, write and pray on this.

Chapter 9

Proverbs 31:30-31

"Charm is deceptive, and beauty does not last, but a woman who fears the Lord will be greatly praised. Reward her for all she has done. Let her deeds publicly declare her praise."
NLT

I feel like the author was writing an "above all" message in these last couple of verses, or something along the lines of "don't forget, please note that…" this statement is really a reminder. A reminder for us women that attraction can be a distraction. Meaning, we ourselves can be so distracted by trying to better our outer appearance, that we forget who God has truly created us to be. Don't get me wrong, I don't think there is anything wrong with beauty and maintaining our own beauty. God created women with beauty that men don't have. The Bible says in 1 Corinthians 11:15, *"And isn't long hair a woman's pride and joy? For it has been given to her as a covering."* NLT. This verse is one of many that show me that God intentionally created a woman the way he did to be beautiful. Women generally care about their hair. It tends to be part of what makes us feel like a woman. That's why the commercials and ads about shampoo focus on the thickness and volume, length and lusciousness of a woman's hair. There's nothing wrong with that. God created us with hair to take care of. However, the physical beauty should never outweigh us taking care of our inward beauty, which is why in the Bible Peter says this:

"Don't be concerned about the outward beauty of fancy hairstyles, expensive jewelry, or beautiful clothes. You should clothe yourselves instead with the beauty that comes from within, the unfading beauty of a gentle and quiet spirit, which is so precious to God." 1

Peter 3:3-4 NLT

The beauty that comes from within is unfading. Everything on the exterior will fade away. But our last two verses in Proverbs 31 says that a woman who fears the Lord will be greatly praised. God wants you to ensure that He is your number one focus. That your relationship and obedience to Him is of utmost priority. When we fear God, which is not being afraid of God but giving Him reverence and choosing to serve Him because He is our master, we will be obedient to Him. Focus on pleasing God. That is what is deserving of praise to God, not our looks.

When I think of some celebrities who are considered "iconic" in this generation, I think about what they represent, and especially with women, a lot of the time, it's sex. They may do great deeds, they may support great causes, but when I look at their social media pages, they are explicitly portraying themselves as a sex symbol. That's what they represent. But, when you become a daughter of the King; a woman who fears the Lord, you represent Jesus Christ. Our last verse says, "let her deeds publicly declare her praise". In other words, let what she does in the public eye, be praised not because of her outward appearance, but may she be praised because of who she is on the inside because that has radiated so strongly towards the outside.

Verse 31 continues to say, "reward her for all she has done." Meaning, hard work deserves to be rewarded! Your hard work, deserves to be acknowledged and rewarded. I don't know what season you're in. Maybe you're a stay-at-home mom, working hard to take care of your kids, or maybe you're finishing up school and about to get your diploma or degree. Perhaps you're working for a church and have been working extra unpaid hours to ensure things are done with excellence. Or, maybe you are retired and figuring out what to do in this new season of your life. Whatever season you're in, know that if anyone has seen your hard work, it's God. He watches, he sees, he takes note. He will reward you for all you have done, my dear sister in Christ. If nobody has told you, I will tell you now, well done. It's not easy to do and to finish strong in something. Hard work pays off and you deserve to be rewarded. I even wish I could treat you, and we can celebrate your hard work in this life! But for now, I hope you have the peace of God to know, that He is well pleased. Those sleepless nights, those nights with the pillow soaked in tears… yet you persevered. Well done.

Verse 31 finishes by saying this, "Let her deeds publicly declare her praise." Your good deeds will speak for itself. You don't have to try to prove yourself to anyone, when you are walking in the will of God, doing what he asked, and doing good deeds. The deeds itself will publicly be seen by others and speak of your praise. Hallelujah.

My dear sister reading this, I would like to pray for you as we come to an end of this study. I hope it has encouraged you, empowered you and enabled you to embrace the idea of continuing to evolve into the virtuous woman that you already are. I encourage you to DO IT. Write that book you've been wanting to write, start learning how to play the guitar, join the gym club you've been saying you want to join, or maybe it's stepping away from something because you feel the need to spend more time with the family. Whatever it is that's been on your mind, I encourage you (also as you pray) that if it's confirmed by the Holy Spirit, to do it. Because you can.

I believe there is so much more in us than we even know ourselves. I believe God wants us to become all that we can be and sometimes that's doing stuff afraid. It's also a continuous reliance and trust in Jesus. But the good news is that we are not alone. He is always with us.

Thank you for your support and reading this book. Let's go out there and be the Proverbs 31 women that God has called us to be! We are in this together! Let's pray.

Heavenly Father,

You deserve all the glory and all the praise. You are holy. Thank you for the opportunity to enter into holiness, just as you are holy because of your dear son, Jesus Christ. I pray for all women reading this, that they would become all they are created to be as virtuous women, here on earth, as it is in heaven. Help them daily, from morning to night, that they may know You are with them. When they feel discouraged, when they feel tempted to give up, may they tangibly feel Your presence, and hear Your still small voice ever so clearly and know you love them, and that your promises are yes and amen. We give you praise. All the glory, all the honor, all the power and all the praise belongs to You. In Jesus name, Amen.

God bless you.

ABOUT THE AUTHOR

Alexandria Nsenga has a Bachelor of Science in Psychiatric Nursing where she began her career as a Psychiatric Nurse in the city of Vancouver, British Columbia. She has vast experience in working in the mental health field and will always have a heart to help those who have experienced trauma. After becoming a mom to her two children, she decided to stay home and focus on raising her two kids and support her husband in pastoral ministry. She is passionate about Jesus and loves the Church. She has been a leader to women through her church and through her Youtube platform and desires to see women encounter Jesus and be everything He has called them to be.

Made in United States
Troutdale, OR
12/05/2023

15416365R00037